CREATING CHARACTERS THAT JUMP OFF THE PAGE

How To Create Memorable And Compelling Characters For Your Novel

HACKNEY AND JONES

Copyright © 2023 by Hackney And Jones

All rights reserved.

No part of this book may be reproduced in any form or by any electronic or mechanical means, including information storage and retrieval systems, without written permission from the author, except for the use of brief quotations in a book review.

Contents

Why Are We Writing This Book?	v
Quick Story	vii
What You Will Get In This Book	ix
Introduction	1
1. Famous Examples Of Compelling Characters	3
2. Myths About Writing Compelling Characters	5
3. Top 10 Questions About Creating Characters	8
4. TYPES OF CHARACTER NEEDED FOR EACH MAIN GENRE	11
Crime	11
Romance	12
Science Fiction	13
Historical Fiction	14
Psychological Thriller	16
Fantasy Fiction	16
5. How To Make Characters More Relatable And Human In A Novel	18
6. MAKING YOUR CHARACTERS 'EMOTIONAL'	20
Emotions	21
7. How To Make Your Characters Unforgettable	24
8. CHARACTER MOTIVATIONS	26
Internal Motivation	27
External Motivation	28
9. The Three-Act Structure	32
10. The Character Arc	33
11. Techniques For Crafting Memorable Characters	43
12. Building Compelling Characters Through Conflict And Emotion	49
13. Putting It All Together To Create A Character Who Jumps Off The Page	54
14. SHOW, DON'T TELL	57
Peter The Detective	58

15. Creating Compelling Villains	66
16. Writing Dialogue For Characters In A Novel	68
17. Examples Of Regrets Your Characters Might Have	70
18. LISTS OF FLAWS, WEAKNESSES AND STRENGTHS	72
Flaws	72
Weaknessess	73
Strengths	74
19. Creating Your Character Arc Using Flaws, Weaknesses And Strengths - The Easy Way!	76
20. Taking It One Step Further	79
21. RESOURCES	85
Character Occupations	88
List Of Vices	90
List Of Good Habits	90
Physical Features	91
22. YOUR FULL CHARACTER PROFILE READY TO GO	92
Basic Information	92
Positive Traits	92
Negative Traits	93
Internal Motivations	93
External Motivations	93
How Does The Character Deal With Change?	94
Conclusion	97
Our Range Of Novel Planning Workbooks	99

Why Are We Writing This Book?

As fiction writers, we understand the importance of crafting unforgettable characters that readers will love. That's why we've spent extra time perfecting the art of character development and want to share our method with you.

In this book, we'll take you through the process of writing compelling characters, from the early stages of character creation to the final touches that will make your characters truly stand out.

Whether you're a seasoned writer or just starting out, we believe that our easy method will help you create characters that will bring your stories to life and leave a lasting impression on your readers.

Quick Story

One thing that really stands out as a lesson for us in creating characters was when we wrote our debut novel **'Meet Me At 10'**.

There was an obvious villain, Kyle and when we first created him, we made him 'bad' all the time. But it was only when we got the notes back from our editor that said that even though he was a villain, villains are still human and humans behave differently in different situations and so if you want to make him believable, have him act differently. So we made sure that on some occasions, he was actually quite pleasant and polite and then other times, he was horrid.

Now when you read **'Meet Me At 10'** you will come across him and remember this story.

Don't make your villains bad – all the time!

What You Will Get In This Book

Here's a brief summary of what you can expect to find inside:

Famous examples of compelling characters: Learn about successful, well-known characters from literature and how their creators developed their unique personalities and motivations.

Myths about writing compelling characters: Discover common misconceptions about character creation and how to avoid falling into these traps.

Top 10 questions about creating characters: Get answers to the most frequently asked questions about crafting believable, dynamic characters.

Types of characters needed for each main genre: Explore the different types of characters that are typically found in different genres, such as romance, mystery, science fiction, and more.

The Character Arc:

Understand the concept of character arc and how to effectively use it to chart a character's development over the course of a story.

Putting it all together:
Find out how to create a complete character profile and the questions you need answered in order to fully flesh out your characters.

Show, don't tell (with examples):
Learn the importance of showing rather than telling in writing and see examples of how to effectively incorporate this technique in your own work.

Overall, this book will provide you with the tools and techniques you need to create compelling, believable characters that will captivate your readers and elevate your writing.

Introduction

IF YOU'RE A WRITER, you know how important it is to create memorable and compelling characters in your fiction. After all, it's the characters that drive the plot and keep readers invested in the story.

BUT CRAFTING dynamic and believable characters can be a challenge. That's why we've put together this guide on **"Creating Characters That Jump Off The Page: How To Create Memorable And Compelling Characters."**

IN THIS BOOK, we'll delve into the character development process and provide you with a variety of techniques and strategies for creating unique and engaging characters that will keep your readers hooked.

ONE THING that sets great fiction apart is the characters.

. . .

THINK about some of your favourite books or movies. Chances are, it's the characters that really stick with you long after you've finished the story. That's because well-developed characters are what make a story come to life. They're what make us care about what happens to them and root for them to succeed.

BUT CREATING memorable and compelling characters is easier said than done. It takes more than just giving your character a cool name and a unique appearance. It requires understanding their motivations, desires, and goals, and using that understanding to craft a fully realised and dynamic character.

IN THIS BOOK, we'll break down the character development process step by step, offering tips and techniques for creating believable and engaging characters that will jump off the page. We'll cover everything from physical descriptions and mannerisms to dialogue and inner monologues. We'll also delve into the role that conflict and emotion play in character development, and how to use these elements to create characters that readers can relate to and empathise with.

WHETHER YOU'RE a seasoned writer or just starting out, we hope this book will provide you with the tools you need to craft unforgettable and compelling characters that will make your fiction stand out. So let's get started on creating some amazing characters.

Famous Examples Of Compelling Characters

Sherlock Holmes from "The Adventures of Sherlock Holmes" by Arthur Conan Doyle:

Sherlock is a brilliant and eccentric detective who is known for his sharp mind, analytical skills, and unconventional methods. He is a compelling character who has fascinated readers for generations.

Atticus Finch from "To Kill a Mockingbird" by Harper Lee:

Atticus is a wise, compassionate, and fair-minded lawyer who is known for his strong sense of justice and moral code. He is a compelling and admirable character who has inspired readers with his wisdom and integrity.

Elizabeth Bennet from "Pride and Prejudice" by Jane Austen:

Elizabeth is a smart, independent, and passionate character who is known for her wit, intelligence, and strong sense of self.

Jay Gatsby from "The Great Gatsby" by F. Scott Fitzgerald:

Gatsby is a wealthy and mysterious man who is obsessed with reclaiming his past love.

Huckleberry Finn from "The Adventures of Huckleberry Finn" by Mark Twain:

This novel is about a young boy who defies societal norms and goes on a journey of self-discovery.

Holden Caulfield from "The Catcher in the Rye" by J.D. Salinger:

This novel is all about a teenage outcast who struggles with the complexities of adulthood.

Ebenezer Scrooge from "A Christmas Carol" by Charles Dickens:

Scrooge is a miserly old man who, after being visited by the ghost of his former business partner and friend, Jacob Marley, is told he will be visited by three spirits, in an attempt to encourage Scrooge to mend his ways.

2

Myths About Writing Compelling Characters

There are several myths about writing compelling characters in a novel that are worth addressing:

Myth: All compelling characters must be perfect or flawless.

Fact: In reality, characters who are too perfect or flawless can be less relatable and less compelling to readers. Characters who are more complex and multifaceted, with flaws and vulnerabilities, can be more relatable and engaging to readers.

Myth: Characters must be likeable to be compelling.

Fact: While likeable characters can be compelling, characters who are unlikable or flawed can also be engaging and interesting to readers. What makes a character compelling is often their depth and complexity, not necessarily their likability.

Myth: Characters must be consistent and unchanging to be compelling.

Fact: In reality, characters who are complex and change over the course of a story can be more compelling to readers. Characters who are consistent and unchanging can be less interesting and less relatable.

By understanding and debunking these myths, writers can more effectively create complex, multifaceted, and compelling characters in their novels

Myth: Characters should be relatable.

Fact: While it's important for readers to be able to connect with characters on some level, it's not necessary for them to be completely relatable. In fact, reading about characters who are different from us can broaden our perspective and help us understand the world in new ways.

Myth: Characters should be well-rounded.

Fact: It's not necessary for all characters to be fully fleshed out and well-rounded. In fact, minor characters or characters who serve a specific purpose in the story can be one-dimensional and still be effective.

Myth: Characters should be realistic.

Fact: It's important for characters to be believable, but it's not necessary for them to be completely realistic. In fiction, it's okay for characters to have extraordinary abilities or experiences that might not be possible in real life.

Myth: Characters should be static.

Fact: Characters can and should change and grow over the course of a story. It's important for them to have arcs and to be dynamic.

Myth: Characters should be original.

Fact: It's not necessary for characters to be completely original and unique. In fact, many well-known and beloved characters are based on archetypes or familiar character types.

Myth: Characters should be fully developed from the start.

Fact: It's not necessary to have a complete understanding of a character before beginning to write. Characters can evolve and change as the story progresses, and it can be a fun and rewarding process to discover new aspects of a character as you write.

Myth: Characters should be based on real people.

Fact: While it can be helpful to draw inspiration from real people, it's important to remember that fictional characters are not real people and should not be treated as such. It's okay to use real people as a starting point, but it's important to give the character their own distinct traits and characteristics.

Myth: Characters should be perfect.

Fact: Perfect characters can be boring to read about. It's okay for characters to have flaws and make mistakes, as long as they are believable and human. In fact, flawed characters can be more relatable and interesting to readers.

3

Top 10 Questions About Creating Characters

How do I create believable and well-rounded characters?
One way to create believable and well-rounded characters is to give them flaws and vulnerabilities, as well as strengths and positive traits. It can also be helpful to give characters distinct motivations and desires, and to think about their backstory and how it has shaped who they are.

How do I create unique and original characters?
To create unique and original characters, consider giving them unusual or unexpected characteristics or traits. It can also be helpful to draw inspiration from real people or from your own life experiences, but be sure to give the character their own distinct personality and voice.

How do I make sure my characters are consistent?
To ensure that your characters are consistent, it can be helpful to create character profiles or sheets that outline their traits, motivations, and goals. This can help you keep track of their characteristics and ensure that their actions and behaviours are consistent with who they are.

How do I make my characters dynamic and change over the course of the story?
To make your characters dynamic, give them goals and desires, and then create obstacles or challenges that they must overcome in order to achieve these goals. As they work to overcome these challenges, your characters will change and grow.

How do I make sure my characters are believable?
To make sure your characters are believable, it can be helpful to do research or draw inspiration from real people. It can also be helpful to give your characters flaws and vulnerabilities, as well as strengths and positive traits, to make them more human and relatable.

How do I make my characters likeable?
To make your characters likeable, give them positive traits and qualities that readers can relate to and admire. It can also be helpful to give them flaws and vulnerabilities, as this can make them more relatable and human.

How do I create realistic characters?
To create realistic characters, it can be helpful to do research or draw inspiration from real people. It's also important to give your characters believable thoughts, emotions, and behaviours, and to consider how they might react in different situations.

How do I create minor characters?
To create minor characters, consider what role they will play in the story and how they will interact with the main characters. It's not necessary for minor characters to be fully fleshed out or well-rounded, but it can be helpful to give them a few distinct characteristics or traits to make them memorable.

How do I create strong and dynamic female characters?
To create strong and dynamic female characters, give them their own goals, desires, and motivations, and make sure they are not just defined by their relationships with male characters. It can also be

helpful to give them flaws and vulnerabilities, as well as strengths and positive traits.

How do I create complex and multidimensional characters?

To create complex and multidimensional characters, give them a variety of traits and characteristics, and consider how these traits might conflict with each other. It can also be helpful to give them internal conflicts or dilemmas to deal with, and to explore their motivations and desires in depth.

4

Types Of Character Needed For Each Main Genre

Crime

In a crime novel, there are several types of characters that you might encounter:

The detective or investigator: This could be the main character in the story, who is responsible for solving the crime or mystery at the heart of the story. They might be a professional detective or investigator, or they might be an amateur sleuth.

The victim: This could be the person who is the target of the crime, or who is the first to discover the crime has been committed. They might be a witness to the crime, or they might be the victim of the crime itself.

The suspect: This could be a character who is suspected of committing the crime, either because they have motive, opportunity, or some other connection to the crime.

The accomplice: This could be a character who assists the suspect in committing the crime, either knowingly or unknowingly.

The witness: This could be a character who sees or knows something about the crime, and who is able to provide information or testimony to the detective or investigator.

The victim's family or friends: This could be a group of characters who are close to the victim and who are affected by the crime in some way. They might be grieving, angry, or seeking justice.

The law enforcement officials: This could be a group of characters who are responsible for investigating and solving the crime, such as police officers, detectives, or forensic experts.

Romance

In a romance novel, there are several types of characters that you might encounter:

The main characters: These are the two primary characters who are central to the romantic plot. They are often referred to as the "hero" and the "heroine," and they are usually the characters who experience the most character development and growth over the course of the story.

The love interest: This could be a character who is initially attracted to one of the main characters and who becomes a romantic rival for their affection.

The supporting characters: These are the secondary characters who play a supporting role in the story, but who are still important to the plot and the development of the main characters. They might be friends, family members, coworkers, or other people in the main characters' lives.

The antagonist: This could be a character who is opposed to the romantic relationship between the main characters and who tries to disrupt or prevent it from happening. They might be motivated by jealousy, envy, or some other personal interest.

The mentor or guide: This could be a character who helps the main characters to navigate the challenges and complications of their romantic relationship, or who offers them advice and support along the way.

The ex-partner: This could be a character who was previously involved with one of the main characters and who is still a part of their life in some way, such as an ex-spouse or an ex-lover.

Science Fiction

In a space opera science fiction novel, there are several types of characters that you might encounter:

The main characters: These are the primary characters who are central to the story and who experience the most character development and growth over the course of the story. They might be humans, aliens, robots, or some other type of being.

The love interest: This could be a character who is initially attracted to one of the main characters and who becomes a romantic rival for their affection.

The supporting characters: These are the secondary characters who play a supporting role in the story, but who are still important to the plot and the development of the main characters. They might be friends, family members, coworkers, or other beings in the main characters' lives.

The antagonist: This could be a character who is opposed to the main characters and who tries to disrupt or prevent them from achieving their goals. They might be motivated by jealousy, envy, or some other personal interest.

The mentor or guide: This could be a character who helps the main characters to navigate the challenges and complications of their journey or mission, or who offers them advice and support along the way.

The ex-partner: This could be a character who was previously involved with one of the main characters and who is still a part of their life in some way, such as an ex-spouse or an ex-lover.

The alien or extraterrestrial beings: In a space opera, there are likely to be many different types of alien or extraterrestrial beings, each with their own unique characteristics, cultures, and motivations.

Historical Fiction

In a historical fiction novel, you might encounter characters who are kings and queens, soldiers, slaves, or other historical figures who played significant roles in the past. Here are a few more examples of the types of characters that you might encounter in a historical fiction novel:

Nobles and aristocracy: These could be characters who are members of the noble or aristocratic class, and who might hold titles such as duke, count, or baron.

Commoners: These could be characters who are not part of the noble or aristocratic class, and who might be merchants, farmers, or artisans.

Religious figures: These could be characters who are members of the clergy, such as priests, bishops, or monks, and who might hold positions of spiritual authority.

Intellectuals and scholars: These could be characters who are learned and educated, and who might be involved in fields such as science, literature, or philosophy.

Political figures: These could be characters who are involved in politics, either as politicians or as advisors, and who might hold positions of power or influence.

Military figures: These could be characters who are involved in the military, either as soldiers, officers, or strategists, and who might be responsible for leading troops or planning battles.

Here are some more ideas:

- A queen who is struggling to hold onto her throne in the face of political intrigue and betrayal.
- A soldier who is struggling to come to terms with the horrors of war and to find his place in the world after returning home.
- A slave who is fighting for her freedom and for the rights of others who are enslaved.
- A duke who is trying to navigate the complicated world of the aristocracy and to maintain his family's status and influence.
- A merchant who is trying to build a successful business and to provide for his family, despite the challenges and competition he faces.
- A priest who is struggling with his faith and his doubts, and who is trying to find his place in the world.
- An intellectual who is trying to make a name for herself in a world that often dismisses or belittles the contributions of women.
- A politician who is trying to balance his personal ambitions with his sense of duty and responsibility to the people he represents.
- A military strategist who is trying to outmanoeuvre his enemies and to protect his country from its foes.

Psychological Thriller

In a psychological thriller, you might encounter characters who are the killer, the victim, and the psychopath. Here are a few more examples of the types of characters that you might encounter in a psychological thriller:

The detective: This could be a character who is responsible for investigating the crime or mystery at the heart of the story.

The witness: This could be a character who saw or heard something that is relevant to the investigation and who is able to provide information or testimony.

The accomplice: This could be a character who is involved in the crime in some way, either as an accomplice or as an accessory.

The victim's family: These could be characters who are related to the victim and who are affected by the crime in some way.

The victim's friends: These could be characters who are friends with the victim and who are affected by the crime in some way.

The victim's co-workers: These could be characters who are coworkers with the victim and who are affected by the crime in some way.

Fantasy Fiction

In fantasy fiction novels, there are a wide range of characters that can be included, depending on the story and the world that the author has created. Some common types of characters that may appear in fantasy fiction include:

Protagonists: The main character or characters of the story, who are often the ones on a quest or journey.

Antagonists: Characters who are in conflict with the protagonist or protagonists, and may be trying to stop them from achieving their goals.

Supporting characters: Characters who play a supporting role in the story and may help or hinder the protagonist on their journey.

Villains: Characters who are the primary antagonists of the story and may be evil or malevolent in some way.

Heroines/heroes: Characters who are brave and courageous, and may play a central role in the story.

Wizards/witches: Characters who have magical abilities or powers.

Creatures: Non-human characters, such as dragons, unicorns, or other mythical beasts.

Royalty: Characters who are members of a royal family or hold a position of power within a kingdom or society.

There are many other types of characters that may appear in fantasy fiction, and the specific characters included in a novel will depend on the story and the world that the author has created.

5

How To Make Characters More Relatable And Human In A Novel

Give them flaws and weaknesses:
No one is perfect, and giving your characters flaws and weaknesses can make them more relatable and human. These could be physical flaws, such as a scar or a disability, or personal flaws, such as insecurity or anger management issues.

Giving your characters emotions and motivations helps to make them more relatable and human:
This could include positive emotions, such as love and joy, or negative emotions, such as anger and sadness. Motivations could include a desire for love, success, or power, or a need to protect or defend something or someone.

Give them relationships and connections:
Giving your characters relationships and connections helps to make them more relatable and human. This could include romantic relationships, friendships, or familial relationships. It could also include connections to a community or a cause.

Give them a sense of identity:
Giving your characters a sense of identity helps to make them more

relatable and human. This could include their values, beliefs, and goals, as well as their personality, habits, and mannerisms.

Give them a backstory:

Giving your characters a backstory helps to make them more relatable and human. This could include their family history, their upbringing, and their experiences that have shaped them.

6

Making Your Characters 'Emotional'

There are several ways that writers can evoke emotion in their characters in novel writing:

Use descriptive language:
Describing a character's thoughts, feelings, and actions in detail can help to convey their emotions to the reader. For example, instead of simply saying that a character is sad, the writer could describe their tears, slumped posture, and lack of appetite to show the reader that the character is sad.

Use dialogue:
Characters' words and the way they speak can convey their emotions to the reader. For example, a character who is angry might speak more loudly or use more aggressive language.

Use body language:
A character's body language can also convey their emotions. For example, a character who is nervous might fidget or avoid eye contact, while a character who is angry might clench their fists or stand with their arms crossed.

Use setting and atmosphere:
The setting and atmosphere of a scene can also help to evoke emotions in the characters. For example, a character might feel overwhelmed and anxious in a crowded, noisy city, while they might feel peaceful and calm in a peaceful, natural setting.

By using these techniques, writers can effectively convey their characters' emotions to the reader and create a more immersive and engaging reading experience.

Emotions

There are many different emotions that a character in a novel might experience, and writers can use a variety of techniques to show these emotions to the reader. Here are some examples of emotions and ways that writers can show them:

Happiness:
A character who is happy might smile, laugh, or exhibit positive body language. They might also use upbeat or positive language and have a more energetic or enthusiastic demeanour.

Sadness:
A character who is sad might cry, have a slumped posture, or exhibit negative body language. They might also use more negative or despondent language and have a slower or more lethargic demeanour.

Anger:
A character who is angry might exhibit aggressive body language, such as clenched fists or a raised voice. They might also use more aggressive or confrontational language and have a more intense or volatile demeanour.

Fear:
A character who is afraid might exhibit fearful body language, such

as trembling or avoiding eye contact. They might also use more anxious or panicked language and have a more anxious or panicked demeanour.

Love:
A character who is in love might exhibit affectionate body language, such as holding hands or gazing into each other's eyes. They might also use more affectionate or loving language and have a more tender or romantic demeanour.

Envy:
A character who is envious might exhibit jealous body language, such as crossing their arms or scowling. They might also use more jealous or resentful language and have a more resentful or bitter demeanour.

Guilt:
A character who feels guilty might exhibit remorseful body language, such as avoiding eye contact or wringing their hands. They might also use more apologetic or self-reproaching language and have a more remorseful or self-conscious demeanour.

Courage:
A character who is brave might exhibit confident body language, such as standing tall or making direct eye contact. They might also use more confident or determined language and have a more assertive or decisive demeanour.

Disgust:
A character who is disgusted might exhibit repelled body language, such as wrinkling their nose or turning away. They might also use more disgusted or revulsed language and have a more repulsed or revolted demeanour.

Hope:
A character who is hopeful might exhibit optimistic body language, such as standing up straight or smiling. They might also use more

optimistic or positive language and have a more positive or upbeat demeanour.

By using these techniques, you can effectively convey your characters' emotions to the reader and create a more immersive and engaging reading experience.

Remember, the key is to create well-rounded and fully realised characters who are believable and relatable to readers. This can help to make your novel more engaging and immersive for your readers.

7

How To Make Your Characters Unforgettable

Here are a few ways you can make your characters truly unforgettable in your novel:

Give your characters distinct and memorable physical features or characteristics:
This could be something as simple as a distinctive hair style or a unique facial feature, or it could be something more unusual like a physical ability or skill.

Give your characters distinct and memorable personalities:
This could involve giving your characters strong opinions, quirks, or mannerisms that set them apart from other characters.

Give your characters compelling backstories:
This could involve giving your characters a history that is interesting, tragic, or inspiring, and that helps to explain who they are and why they act the way they do.

Give your characters clear motivations, goals, and desires:

This could involve giving your characters a clear purpose or drive that shapes their actions and decisions.

Give your characters meaningful and significant roles in the story:
This could involve giving your characters important plot functions or relationships that make them integral to the story.

By following these tips, you can create characters that are distinct, memorable, and compelling, and that will stay with readers long after they have finished your novel.

8

Character Motivations

Here are a few examples of interesting motivations for characters in a novel:

A desire for love and connection:
This could be a character who is seeking love and connection with others, whether it's romantic love, familial love, or platonic love.

A desire for success and achievement:
This could be a character who is driven to succeed and achieve their goals, whether it's in their career, their personal life, or their relationships.

A desire for power and control:
This could be a character who is seeking power and control over their own life or the lives of others.

A need to protect and defend:
This could be a character who is motivated by a sense of duty or responsibility to protect and defend someone or something that they care about.

A desire for revenge:
This could be a character who is motivated by a desire for revenge against someone who has wronged them or someone they care about.

A desire for redemption:
This could be a character who is seeking redemption for past mistakes or misdeeds.

A desire for self-discovery:
This could be a character who is seeking self-discovery and personal growth.

Internal Motivation

Internal motivation refers to the driving forces or factors that come from within an individual. It is the desire or drive to do something that comes from within, rather than being motivated by external factors or rewards. Internal motivation can be driven by personal values, goals, or beliefs, and it can be a powerful force in shaping an individual's behavior and actions.

Some examples of internal motivation might include a desire to achieve personal growth, to improve oneself, or to fulfil a personal dream or ambition. Internal motivation can be a strong and sustained force, as it is driven by an individual's own personal desires and goals

Examples:

Here are five examples of internal motivation that a character in a novel might have:

- **Personal growth:** A character might be internally motivated to learn and grow as an individual, seeking

out new experiences and challenges in order to become a better version of themselves.
- **Self-improvement:** A character might be internally motivated to work on their weaknesses or flaws in order to become a more well-rounded and successful person.
- **Fulfilling a dream or ambition:** A character might be internally motivated to pursue a particular dream or ambition, driven by a deep desire to achieve a specific goal.
- **Personal values:** A character might be internally motivated by their personal values and beliefs, such as a commitment to justice, honesty, or compassion.
- **Overcoming personal challenges:** A character might be internally motivated to overcome personal challenges or obstacles in order to become a stronger and more resilient person.

By identifying and exploring a character's internal motivations, writers can create more complex and multi-dimensional characters who are driven by their own personal desires and goals.

External Motivation

External motivation refers to the driving forces or factors that come from outside an individual. It is the desire or drive to do something that is motivated by external rewards or incentives, rather than being driven by internal factors or personal goals.

External motivation can take many forms, such as the desire for material rewards, recognition or status, or a sense of obligation or responsibility to others. External motivation can be a powerful force, as it can provide incentives and rewards that can motivate an individual to take action.

However, external motivation can also be less sustainable than internal motivation, as it relies on external factors and can be less deeply ingrained in an individual's personal values and goals

Examples:

Here are five examples of external motivation:

- **Material rewards:** A character might be motivated by the desire for material rewards, such as money, possessions, or privileges.
- **Recognition or status:** A character might be motivated by the desire for recognition or status, such as the desire to be praised, admired, or respected by others.
- **Social pressure or obligation:** A character might be motivated by social pressure or a sense of obligation to others, such as a sense of duty to family, friends, or community.
- **Competition:** A character might be motivated by the desire to win or succeed in competition, driven by a desire to outperform others or achieve a particular goal.
- **Rewards or incentives:** A character might be motivated by the promise of rewards or incentives, such as promotions, bonuses, or privileges.

Remember, the key is to create believable and well-rounded characters who have motivations that drive their actions and shape their journey or arc in the story:

- **Nervous habits:** This could be a character who constantly fiddles with their hair, bites their nails, or taps their foot when they are anxious or stressed.
- **Unique speech patterns:** This could be a character who speaks with a distinct accent, uses unusual words or phrases, or talks very fast or very slowly.
- **Physical tics:** This could be a character who has a physical tic, such as a twitch, stutter, or stammer, that is noticeable when they speak or interact with others.

- **Gestures or body language:** This could be a character who has distinctive gestures or body language, such as a habit of shrugging their shoulders, crossing their arms, or avoiding eye contact.
- **Unique dress or fashion sense:** This could be a character who always wears a specific type of clothing or accessory, or who has a distinctive or unusual style.

Remember, the key is to use unique mannerisms sparingly and only when they serve a purpose in revealing something important about the character. Too many unnecessary details can distract from the main plot and make your character feel unrealistic or unbelievable.

Here are a few examples of compelling secrets that a character might have to keep in a novel:

- **A dark past:** This could be a character who has a criminal record, a history of abuse, or some other type of dark or traumatic past that they are trying to keep hidden.
- **A family secret:** This could be a character who is keeping a secret about their family, such as a hidden parent, an illegitimate sibling, or a family member with a dark or shameful past.
- **A secret identity:** This could be a character who is keeping their true identity hidden for some reason, such as an undercover detective, a spy, or someone who is in witness protection.
- **A secret talent or ability:** This could be a character who has a unique or unusual talent or ability, such as telepathy, telekinesis, or the ability to communicate with animals, that they are trying to keep hidden.
- **A secret relationship:** This could be a character who is in a secret or forbidden relationship, such as a secret affair, a same-sex relationship, or a relationship with someone who is considered off-limits.
- **A character facing a physical challenge or**

obstacle: This could be something like a character trying to survive in a dangerous or hostile environment, or a character trying to overcome a physical disability or injury.
- **A character facing conflict with another character:** This could be a character who is in competition with another character for something, or a character who is at odds with another character due to conflicting goals or values.
- **A character facing conflict with society or the environment:** This could be a character who is struggling to fit in with their community or society, or a character who is facing challenges due to the environment in which they live.
- **A character dealing with external struggles related to their career or social status:** This could be a character who is trying to succeed in a competitive field, or a character who is struggling to overcome a lack of resources or privilege.
- **A character facing external conflict related to the plot:** This could be a character who is trying to solve a mystery, prevent a disaster, or achieve a specific goal, and is facing external obstacles or challenges in the process.

The key is to create an external conflict that is meaningful and relevant to the character's overall arc and development, and that helps to drive the plot and create tension.

9

The Three-Act Structure

The three-act structure is a storytelling model that is often used in fiction, including novels, movies, and plays. It is a way of dividing a story into three distinct parts, each with its own purpose and function.

The first act, also known as the setup, introduces the main characters and setting, as well as the main conflict or problem that will drive the story. This act sets the stage for the rest of the story and establishes the key elements and themes.

The second act, also known as the confrontation, is where the main conflict or problem comes to a head and the characters are forced to deal with it. This act is typically the longest and most complex, and it involves the characters facing challenges and obstacles as they try to resolve the main conflict. We often say this is the 'changing' of the characters.

The third act, also known as the resolution, is where the main conflict is finally resolved and the story reaches its conclusion. This act typically involves the characters achieving their goals or finding a resolution to the main conflict.

10

The Character Arc

A character arc is the progression of a character's development over the course of a story. It can be as simple as a character learning an important lesson or growing in some way, or it can be more complex, involving multiple stages of change and growth.

As an important element of character development, a character arc helps to add depth and meaning to a character, making them more dynamic and believable. A character arc can be used to show how a character grows or changes as a result of their experiences and interactions in the story. It can also be used to highlight the internal conflicts and struggles that a character faces and how they overcome them.

In short, a character arc is a way of showing the transformation of a character over the course of a story, and it is an essential element of good character development.

Here are a few examples of famous movies with character arcs:

"The Lion King" - In this animated classic, young lion cub Simba goes through a significant character arc as he grapples with the responsibilities of becoming king and learns to overcome his own fears and doubts.

"Rocky" - The titular character of "Rocky" goes through a classic hero's journey arc as he overcomes seemingly insurmountable odds to become a successful boxer.

"The Shawshank Redemption" - In this drama, the character of Andy Dufresne goes through a transformation from a timid and defeated man to a confident and successful individual, thanks to his friendship with fellow inmate Red.

"The Dark Knight" - The character of Batman in "The Dark Knight" goes through a significant character arc as he grapples with the difficult choices he must make in his quest to protect Gotham City.

"Toy Story" - In the "Toy Story" franchise, the character of Woody goes through a character arc as he learns to embrace change and accept the fact that his place as Andy's favourite toy is no longer secure.

Here are a few examples of famous books with great character arcs:

"To Kill a Mockingbird" - In this classic novel, the character of Scout Finch undergoes a transformation as she learns about the injustices of the world and the importance of standing up for what is right.

"Pride and Prejudice" - In "Pride and Prejudice," the character of Elizabeth Bennet undergoes a character arc as she learns to overcome her pride and judgmental nature and finds true love.

"The Great Gatsby" - The titular character of "The Great

Gatsby" goes through a significant character arc as he grapples with his past and his unrequited love for Daisy.

"The Catcher in the Rye" - In "The Catcher in the Rye," the character of Holden Caulfield undergoes a character arc as he grapples with the loss of his brother and his own feelings of alienation and disillusionment.

"The Alchemist" - In "The Alchemist," the character of Santiago undergoes a transformation as he embarks on a journey of self-discovery and learns to pursue his dreams.

Creating a character arc for a novel involves several steps:

1. **Determine the character's starting point:** Before you can create a character arc, you need to know where your character is starting from. This might involve understanding their background, personality, and motivations.
2. **Identify the character's goal or desire:** A character arc is driven by the character's desire or goal. This could be something external, like a desire for success or love, or it could be something internal, like a desire for personal growth or self-improvement.
3. **Create conflict and challenges:** In order for a character arc to be meaningful and impactful, the character must face challenges and obstacles. These can be external, such as external forces working against the character, or internal, such as the character's own flaws or personal struggles.
4. **Show the character's growth and development:** As the character faces challenges and conflicts, they should undergo some sort of growth or development. This could involve learning an important lesson, changing their perspective, or growing as a person in some way.

5. **Reach the resolution:** The character arc should ultimately lead to some sort of resolution, whether that be the character achieving their goal or coming to some sort of realisation or understanding.

In summary, creating a character arc involves determining the character's starting point, identifying their goal or desire, creating conflict and challenges, showing their growth and development, and reaching a resolution. By following these steps, you can craft a meaningful and impactful character arc for your novel.

Here are a few examples of <u>starting points</u> for a character arc:

1. **The character is in a state of denial or avoidance:** Perhaps the character is in a state of denial about an important issue or problem in their life. They might be avoiding facing a difficult situation or dealing with their own flaws.
2. **The character is stuck in a rut:** Maybe the character feels stagnant or unfulfilled in their current situation. They might be bored, unhappy, or unfulfilled in their career or personal life.
3. **The character is at a crossroads:** The character might be facing a difficult choice or decision that will significantly impact their future. They might be trying to choose between two different paths or opportunities.
4. **The character is struggling with a personal flaw or weakness:** Perhaps the character is struggling with a personal flaw or weakness that is holding them back in some way. They might be trying to overcome a fear, addiction, or other issue.
5. **The character is dealing with a significant loss or change:** The character might be dealing with the aftermath of a significant loss or change in their life, such as the loss of a loved one or a major career change.

The key is to **identify a starting point** that provides a clear and meaningful catalyst for the character's development and growth over the course of the story

Here are a few examples of a character arc for a character who is shy and poor:

Overcoming shyness: In this arc, the character starts out as very shy and introverted, and they struggle to express themselves or make friends. Over the course of the story, they learn to overcome their shyness and become more confident and self-assured. This could involve finding a supportive group of friends, learning new skills or hobbies, or facing their fears and insecurities.

Escaping poverty: In this arc, the character starts out living in poverty and struggling to make ends meet. Over the course of the story, they work to overcome their financial struggles and achieve financial independence. This could involve finding a better job, learning new skills, or starting a business.

Finding self-worth: In this arc, the character starts out feeling like they don't matter or that they don't have any value. Over the course of the story, they learn to appreciate themselves and their own worth, and they become more confident and self-assured. This could involve learning new skills or hobbies, finding a supportive group of friends, or achieving a personal goal.

Overcoming adversity: In this arc, the character starts out facing significant challenges or obstacles, such as poverty, shyness, or discrimination. Over the course of the story, they work to overcome these challenges and emerge stronger and more resilient.

It's the JOURNEY that makes it compelling.

Here are a few examples of a character arc for a character who is stubborn and rich:

Learning to compromise: In this arc, the character starts out as very stubborn and unwilling to consider the perspectives or needs of others. Over the course of the story, they learn to compromise and become more open-minded and considerate. This could involve facing challenges that force them to see things in a new way, or finding a supportive group of friends or mentors who help them to see things differently.

Finding humility: In this arc, the character starts out as very arrogant and self-absorbed, and they struggle to see the value in others. Over the course of the story, they learn to be more humble and to appreciate the worth of others or learning to put the needs of others before their own.

Overcoming entitlement: In this arc, the character starts out feeling entitled to everything they want, and they struggle to understand the value of hard work or sacrifice. Over the course of the story, they learn to overcome their sense of entitlement and become more responsible and self-sufficient and learning to appreciate the things they have rather than constantly striving for more.

Finding purpose: In this arc, the character starts out feeling aimless and directionless, and they struggle to find meaning or purpose in their life. Over the course of the story, they discover a passion or cause that gives their life meaning, and they become more focused and driven.

Here are a few examples of a character arc for a character who is hiding that they have a criminal record and are illusive:

Overcoming a criminal past: In this arc, the character starts out hiding their criminal record and living in fear of being discovered. Over the course of the story, they work to overcome their past and become a better person, perhaps by seeking redemption, making amends, or finding a new purpose in life.

Finding the courage to reveal their past: In this arc, the character starts out hiding their criminal record out of fear or shame, and they struggle to be honest with others about who they are. Over the course of the story, they find the courage to reveal their past and confront the consequences of their actions.

Redefining their identity: In this arc, the character starts out hiding their criminal record and trying to escape their past, and they struggle to define who they are and what they want in life. Over the course of the story, they work to redefine their identity and find a new sense of purpose and direction.

Facing the consequences of their actions: In this arc, the character starts out hiding their criminal record and trying to avoid the consequences of their actions, but eventually they are forced to confront the reality of what they have done. This could involve facing legal consequences, dealing with the aftermath of their actions, or finding a way to make amends.

There are many different sources that you can use to get character names for a novel. Here are a few ideas:

Baby name websites: There are many websites that provide lists of baby names sorted by various criteria, such as popularity, origin, or meaning. These can be a great source of inspiration for character names.

Online name generators: There are many online name generators that can help you to generate random names or names based on specific criteria. Some of these tools allow you to specify parameters such as the gender of the character, the origin of the name, or the type of name you are looking for.

Phone books: Phone books can be a great source of character names, particularly if you are looking for names that are common or traditional in a specific region.

Books of names: There are many books available that provide lists of names sorted by various criteria, such as popularity, origin, or meaning. These books can be a helpful resource for finding unique or unusual names.

Historical records: Historical records, such as census data or birth records, can be a good source of character names that are appropriate for a specific time period or location.

Remember, the key is to choose a name that is <u>appropriate </u>for your character and genre and that helps to reveal something about their personality or background.

Here are some examples of a character arc for a character going from shy to confident, including the stages they go through:

The beginning: The character is shy, introverted, and lacks self-confidence. They may struggle to speak up for themselves or to express their opinions and feelings. They may also avoid social situations or feel anxious in groups.

The middle: The character begins to confront and challenge their own insecurities and self-doubt. They may seek out new experiences or take risks that push them outside of their comfort zone. They may also seek support and guidance from friends, family, or a mentor. They may be forced to face a situation they think they will fail at, but discover a strength.

The end: The character becomes more confident and self-assured. They may assert themselves more in social situations and become more vocal and expressive. They may also take on leadership roles or pursue their passions and goals with greater determination.

Of course, this is just one example of a character arc, and there are many different ways that a character could go from shy to confident. The key is to show the character's growth and development in a believable and authentic way, and to give them the opportunity to overcome challenges and obstacles as they work towards their goal of becoming more confident.

Here are some examples of a character arc for a character going from rude and selfish to kind, including the stages they go through:

The beginning: The character is rude and selfish, and they may put their own needs and desires above those of others. They may be insensitive or thoughtless in their interactions with others, and they may not think about the consequences of their actions.

The middle: The character begins to realise the negative impact of their behavior on others and starts to reflect on their own motivations and values. They may seek out opportunities to help others or to make amends for their past mistakes. They may also seek guidance or support from others as they try to change their behaviour.

The end: The character becomes kind and selfless, and they are able to put the needs of others before their own. They may become more empathetic and compassionate, and they may be more considerate and thoughtful in their interactions with others.

Here are some examples of an interesting character profile for a character going from rude and selfish to kind:

Name: Samantha
Age: 25
Occupation: Sales representative

Samantha is a rude and selfish young woman who is always looking out for herself and doesn't care about the feelings or needs of others. She is impatient, critical, and quick to anger, and she doesn't think twice about trampling over others to get what she wants.

However, after a series of confrontations and setbacks, Samantha begins to realise the negative impact of her behaviour on others and starts to reflect on her own motivations and values. She begins to seek out opportunities to help others and to make amends for her past mistakes, and she starts to become more empathetic and compassionate.

By the end of her journey, Samantha has transformed into a kind and selfless person who is able to put the needs of others before her own.

Name: Jake
Age: 40
Occupation: Corporate lawyer

Jake is a rude and selfish corporate lawyer who is always looking out for his own interests and doesn't care about the impact of his actions on others. He is arrogant, self-absorbed, and quick to anger, and he doesn't think twice about stepping on others to get ahead.

However, after a series of confrontations and setbacks, Jake begins to realise the negative impact of his behaviour on others and starts to reflect on his own motivations and values. He begins to seek out opportunities to help others and to make amends for his past mistakes, and he starts to become more empathetic and compassionate.

By the end of his journey, Jake has transformed into a kind and selfless person who is able to put the needs of others before his own.

11

Techniques For Crafting Memorable Characters

In this chapter, we'll be discussing some of the key elements that go into creating dynamic and believable characters that will jump off the page.

One important element of character development is the use of physical descriptions and mannerisms. These details help to bring your characters to life and make them feel more real and distinct. Physical descriptions can include things like appearance, clothing, and body language. Mannerisms, on the other hand, are habits or behaviours that a character exhibits. Both of these elements can be used to add depth and personality to your characters and make them more memorable and engaging.

Another important element of character development is giving your characters unique voices and personalities. This includes the way they talk, their mannerisms and behaviours, and their overall demeanour. Giving your characters unique voices and personalities helps to make them stand out and feel more distinct, which can be especially important if you have a large cast of characters.

Finally, creating engaging dialogue and inner monologues is essential for bringing your characters to life and making them feel believable. Dialogue is the way that characters communicate with each other, and it can be used to reveal character traits, advance the plot, and create tension. Inner monologues, on the other hand, are the thoughts and feelings that a character has but does not express aloud. These can be especially helpful for revealing a character's motivations, desires, and fears.

In summary, crafting memorable characters involves using physical descriptions and mannerisms to bring them to life, giving them unique voices and personalities, and creating engaging dialogue and inner monologues. By following these techniques, you can create dynamic and believable characters that will engage and captivate your readers

Here are a few examples of physical descriptions that you could use in a novel:

1. **Appearance:** This could include things like hair colour and style, facial features, body type, and other physical characteristics.
2. **Clothing:** The clothes that a character wears can reveal a lot about their personality and social status.
3. **Body language:** This includes things like posture, gestures, and facial expressions, which can all convey important information about a character.
4. **Mannerisms:** This could include habits or behaviours such as fidgeting, biting their nails, or tapping their foot, which can help to make a character feel more distinct and believable.

Remember, the key is to use physical descriptions and mannerisms sparingly and only when they serve a purpose in revealing something important about the character. Too many unnecessary details can bog down the story and distract from the main plot.

There are several ways to make your characters stand out in a novel:

1. **Give them unique and distinct personalities:** One way to make your characters stand out is to give them unique and distinct personalities. This could involve giving them distinct mannerisms, behaviours, and speaking styles, as well as incorporating their own goals, desires, and flaws.
2. **Use physical descriptions and mannerisms sparingly:** While physical descriptions and mannerisms can be helpful for bringing your characters to life, it's important to use them sparingly and only when they serve a purpose. Too many unnecessary details can distract from the main plot and make your characters feel flat and unmemorable.
3. **Develop their backstories:** Giving your characters a rich and detailed backstory can help to make them feel more fully realised and believable. This could involve exploring their relationships, experiences, and motivations, which can all help to make them stand out and feel distinct.
4. **Use dialogue and inner monologues to reveal character traits:** Dialogue and inner monologues can be powerful tools for revealing character traits and making your characters feel more distinct. By using unique and distinct speaking styles and incorporating the characters' thoughts and feelings, you can make your characters stand out and feel more believable.
5. **Create interesting and complex conflicts:** Another way to make your characters stand out is to create interesting and complex conflicts for them to solve.

Here are a few unusual physical characteristics that you could give to a character in a novel:

1. **Unusual hair colour or style:** This could be something like bright pink hair, green hair, or a distinctive haircut.
2. **Unusual facial features:** This could be something like a large or small nose, pronounced cheekbones, or a distinctive scar.
3. **Unusual body type:** This could be a character who is very tall, very short, or has a unique body shape.
4. **Unusual skin colour or texture:** This could be a character who has a very pale or very dark complexion, or a character who has a unique skin condition or texture.
5. **Unusual physical abilities or skills:** This could be a character who has exceptional strength, agility, or coordination, or a character who has a unique physical ability or skill.

Use unusual physical characteristics sparingly and only when they serve a purpose in revealing something important about the character. Too many unnecessary details can distract from the main plot and make your character feel unrealistic or unbelievable

Here are a few unusual hobbies that you could give to a character in a novel:

1. **Competitive juggling:** This could be a character who is passionate about juggling and takes part in juggling competitions.
2. **Collecting rare or unusual items:** This could be a character who collects things like old coins, stamps, or obscure artefacts.
3. **Extreme sports:** This could be a character who enjoys activities like skydiving, bungee jumping, or rock climbing.
4. **Cosplay:** This could be a character who enjoys creating and wearing elaborate costumes based on their favourite characters or franchises.

5. **Urban exploration:** This could be a character who enjoys exploring abandoned buildings or urban areas and documenting their findings.
6. **Beekeeping:** This could be a character who is passionate about bees and keeps a hive in their backyard.
7. **Knitting:** This could be a character who is an avid knitter and enjoys creating unique and intricate projects.

The key is to choose a hobby that is interesting and unique, and that helps to reveal something about the character's personality or interests.

Here are a few examples of interesting job titles that you could give to a character in a novel:

1. **Cryptozoologist:** This could be a character who studies and investigates mythical or legendary creatures, such as Bigfoot or the Loch Ness Monster.
2. **Professional gamer:** This could be a character who makes a living by competing in video game tournaments.
3. **Ghost hunter:** This could be a character who investigates paranormal activity and tries to communicate with ghosts.
4. **Space tourist:** This could be a character who pays to travel to space for leisure or adventure.
5. **Food critic:** This could be a character who writes reviews or articles about restaurants and food for a living.
6. **Illusionist:** This could be a character who performs magic tricks and illusions for a living.
7. **Private investigator:** This could be a character who is hired to investigate crimes or solve mysteries.

Choose a job title that is unique and that helps to reveal something about the character's personality or interests

Here are five examples of interesting backstories for a character in a novel:

1. **A character who experienced a major loss or tragedy:** This could be the loss of a loved one, the loss of a home or possessions, or any other significant loss that has had a profound impact on the character's life.
2. **A character who has overcome a major obstacle or challenge:** This could be something like overcoming a physical disability or overcoming a difficult period in their life.
3. **A character who has lived a life of privilege:** This could be a character who has always had everything they could want, and as a result, has never had to work hard for anything.
4. **A character who has lived a life of poverty:** This could be a character who has always struggled to make ends meet and has had to work hard to survive.
5. **A character who has lived in multiple cultures:** This could be a character who has lived in multiple countries or has experienced different cultures in some other way, and as a result, has a unique perspective on the world.

Try to create a backstory that is rich and detailed, and that helps to give your character depth and complexity.

12

Building Compelling Characters Through Conflict And Emotion

Internal conflict is a struggle that a character faces within themselves, such as a conflict of desires, values, or morals. It can be driven by a character's own thoughts, feelings, or beliefs, and it typically relates to the character's inner world or psychological state.

External conflict, on the other hand, is a struggle that a character faces with external forces or circumstances. It can involve conflicts with other characters, conflicts with the environment or society, or conflicts with external obstacles or challenges. External conflict typically relates to the character's interactions with the outside world and can be driven by external factors such as plot, setting, or other characters.

Both internal and external conflict are important elements of character development, and they can be used together to create dynamic and compelling characters. Internal conflict can help to reveal a character's inner thoughts, feelings, and motivations, while external conflict can help to drive the plot and give characters the opportunity to grow and change. By using both internal and external conflict in your story, you can create complex and believable characters that are engaging and relatable to readers.

Here are a few examples of internal conflicts that a character might face in a novel:

A character struggling with their own desires or goals: This could be a character who wants to follow their dreams but is afraid of failure, or a character who wants to make a major life change but is hesitant to take the risk.

A character grappling with their own morals or values: This could be a character who is torn between two conflicting values, or a character who is struggling to reconcile their actions with their own personal code of ethics.

A character dealing with self-doubt or insecurity: This could be a character who is struggling to believe in themselves or their own abilities, or a character who is grappling with low self-esteem.

A character facing an internal conflict between their head and their heart: This could be a character who is struggling to choose between two conflicting desires or goals, or a character who is torn between their logical side and their emotional side.

A character dealing with an internal struggle related to their past: This could be a character who is trying to come to terms with a traumatic event from their past, or a character who is struggling to move on from a difficult period in their life.

The important thing is to create an internal conflict that is meaningful and relevant to the character's overall arc and development.

Here are a few examples of external conflicts that a character might face in a novel:

A character facing a physical challenge or obstacle: This could be something like a character trying to survive in a dangerous or hostile environment, or a character trying to overcome a physical disability or injury.

A character facing conflict with another character: This could be a character who is in competition with another character for something, or a character who is at odds with another character due to conflicting goals or values.

A character facing conflict with society or the environment: This could be a character who is struggling to fit in with their community or society, or a character who is facing challenges due to the environment in which they live.

A character dealing with external struggles related to their career or social status: This could be a character who is trying to succeed in a competitive field, or a character who is struggling to overcome a lack of resources or privilege.

A character facing external conflict related to the plot: This could be a character who is trying to solve a mystery, prevent a disaster, or achieve a specific goal, and is facing external obstacles or challenges in the process.

Adding flaws to your characters can make them more interesting and compelling because it helps to make them feel more real and relatable to readers. Flaws can help to make your characters feel more human and believable, and they can add depth and complexity to your story.

When a character is too perfect or flawless, they can feel unrealistic and unrelatable to readers. Flaws help to balance out a character's strengths and give them a more human and believable quality. They also provide opportunities for character growth and development, as a character's flaws can be a source of conflict or challenges that they have to overcome.

In addition, flaws can help to make your characters more relatable to readers. By giving your characters flaws that are common or universal, such as insecurity, jealousy, or anger, you can create a connection with your readers and help them to identify with your characters.

Overall, adding flaws to your characters can make them more interesting and compelling by making them feel more real and relatable, and by providing opportunities for character growth and development. So, it is a good idea to include flaws in your characters as it can help to make your story more interesting and engaging.

Here are a few examples of flaws that you could give to a character in a novel:

Pride: This could be a character who is overly confident or self-assured, and who has difficulty admitting when they are wrong or need help.

Greed: This could be a character who is overly focused on material possessions or wealth, and who is willing to do whatever it takes to acquire more.

Jealousy: This could be a character who is prone to feelings of envy or resentment towards others, and who struggles with feelings of inadequacy.

Anger: This could be a character who has difficulty controlling their temper and tends to react impulsively when they are upset.

Insecurity: This could be a character who lacks confidence in themselves or their abilities, and who struggles with self-doubt.

Impatience: This could be a character who is prone to impatience and has difficulty waiting for things to happen.

Selfishness: This could be a character who is overly focused on their own needs and desires, and who has difficulty considering the needs of others.

Aim to choose a flaw that is appropriate for your character and that helps to reveal something about their personality or background. Flaws can help to make your characters feel more relatable and believable, and they can add depth and complexity to your story

13

Putting It All Together To Create A Character Who Jumps Off The Page

To help you with this, we have provided an example below:

Genre: Crime

Pick the character you will focus on: The lead detective.

Name: Peter

Age: 45

Flaws: Struggles with self-doubt and can be overly critical of himself, prone to overworking and neglecting his personal life.

Physical characteristics: Tall and lean, with salt-and-pepper hair and piercing green eyes. Has a scar above his left eyebrow from a case gone wrong.

Values and beliefs: Believes in justice and is fiercely committed to solving cases and bringing perpetrators to justice. Has a strong moral code and will go to great lengths to protect the innocent.

Background: A seasoned detective with over 20 years of experience, he has seen it all and is known for his sharp mind and relentless pursuit of the truth. Despite his flaws, he is highly respected by his colleagues and is often called upon to lead complex and high-profile cases. He has a deep love for his family and a close group of friends, but his dedication to his work often comes at the expense of his personal relationships.

Peter's internal motivation: This could be his strong belief in justice and his desire to protect the innocent. He is fiercely committed to solving cases and bringing perpetrators to justice, and this drive comes from a deep-seated belief in the importance of justice. He may also be motivated by a desire to prove himself and overcome his self-doubt, as he struggles with self-doubt and can be overly critical of himself.

Peter's external motivation: This could be his desire to be respected and valued by his colleagues and superiors. As a seasoned detective with a strong reputation, he is often called upon to lead complex and high-profile cases, and he may be motivated by the desire to maintain his reputation and be seen as a valuable member of the team. He may also be motivated by his love for his family and close group of friends, and his desire to maintain and strengthen these relationships despite the demands of his work

Here is a possible character arc for Peter in a crime novel:

Act 1: In the beginning of the story, Peter is a seasoned detective who is highly respected by his colleagues and known for his sharp mind and relentless pursuit of the truth. Despite his flaws, he is deeply committed to justice and protecting the innocent. However, he is struggling with self-doubt and is prone to overworking, causing him to neglect his personal relationships.

Act 2: As the story progresses, Peter becomes more and more invested in solving the case and bringing the perpetrators to justice. His drive to succeed and his commitment to justice begin to consume him, causing him to neglect his personal relationships even more. He becomes more critical of himself and starts to struggle with feelings of self-doubt and inadequacy.

Act 3: As the case ends, Peter realises the toll that his dedication to his work has taken on his personal life. He begins to re-evaluate his priorities and try to balance his work and personal relationships. He learns to let go of his self-doubt and become more confident in his abilities as a detective. Through this process, he grows as a character and becomes more well-rounded and self-aware.

As you can see, by fleshing out this character with as much information as we can add, "Peter" jumps off the page to a point where we feel like we know him in real life. We can picture him almost - maybe even have someone in our real life that reminds us of Peter? If you can describe your characters with as much depth and detail as possible, giving them back stories and internal/external motivations, you will write scenes that involve them with more authenticity, and your reader will become more invested in the story.

14

Show, Don't Tell

"Show, don't tell" is a common piece of advice for writers, and it refers to the idea of using descriptive language and actions to show the reader what is happening, rather than simply telling them what is happening.

For example, instead of telling the reader that a character is angry, the writer might describe the character's body language and actions (such as clenched fists or a raised voice) to show the reader that the character is angry. This allows the reader to experience the scene and events in a more immersive and engaging way, rather than just being told about them.

Using "show, don't tell" in writing can help to create a more vivid and dynamic reading experience, and can also help to reveal character and plot in a more subtle and effective way. It is a useful technique for writers to keep in mind when crafting their stories and characters

Here are some examples of how "show, don't tell" can be used in novels:

Instead of telling the reader that a character is sad, the writer might describe the character's slumped posture, tears, and lack of appetite to show the reader that the character is sad.

Example: *"Sarah sat at the kitchen table, staring blankly at the plate of food in front of her. She hadn't touched it since it was placed in front of her, and her eyes were red and puffy from crying. It was clear to anyone who looked at her that she was devastated."*

Instead of telling the reader that a character is angry, the writer might describe the character's clenched fists, raised voice, or aggressive body language to show the reader that the character is angry.

Example: *"John's face turned red with anger as he slammed his fist on the table. "I can't believe you would do this to me!" he shouted, his voice rising with each word. It was clear that he was livid."*

Instead of telling the reader that a character is afraid, the writer might describe the character's rapid breathing, wide eyes, or trembling to show the reader that the character is afraid.

Example: *"As the car raced down the dark, winding road, Maria's hands began to shake. She could feel her heart pounding in her chest, and she struggled to catch her breath. She was terrified."*

Using "show, don't tell" in writing can help to create a more immersive and engaging reading experience, and can also help to reveal character and plot in a more subtle and effective way. It is a useful technique for writers to keep in mind when crafting their stories and characters

Peter The Detective

ACT 1:
Here are some examples of how "show, don't tell" could be used to illustrate Peter's character arc in Act 1:

Instead of telling the reader that Peter is struggling with self-doubt, the writer might describe his hesitation and second-guessing as he approaches a crime scene, or his tendency to seek reassurance from his colleagues before making a decision.

Example: *"Peter stood at the edge of the crime scene, staring at the body in front of him. He took a deep breath and tried to push aside the nagging doubts in his mind. He had been a detective for over 20 years, but he still struggled with self-doubt from time to time. He turned to his colleague, a hint of desperation in his voice. "Do you think I'm making the right call here?"*

Instead of telling the reader that Peter is prone to overworking, the writer might describe his tendency to bring work home with him, or his reluctance to take breaks or days off.

Example: *"Peter sat at his kitchen table, surrounded by stacks of files and case notes. He had been working on this case for days, barely taking a break to eat or sleep. He was determined to solve it, no matter the cost. His family and friends had stopped trying to get him to take a break – they knew he was driven, and he was always focused on his work."*

Instead of telling the reader that Peter neglects his personal relationships, the writer might describe his tendency to cancel plans with friends and family, or his lack of communication with them when he is wrapped up in a case.

Example: *"Peter glanced at his phone, scrolling through the missed calls and messages from his family and friends. He had been so wrapped up in this case that he hadn't even realised how long it had been since he had last spoken to them."*

ACT 2:

"Show, don't tell" can be used to illustrate Peter's character arc in Act 2. Here are some examples of how this could be done:

Instead of telling the reader that Peter becomes more invested in solving the case, the writer might describe his increased focus and dedication to the case, such as spending longer hours at the office or refusing to take time off.

Example: *"Peter's office was a mess of papers and empty coffee cups. He had been working on this case for weeks, and he was starting to lose track of time. He was consumed by his drive to succeed and bring the perpetrators to justice, and he refused to take a break until the case was solved. His colleagues had stopped trying to get him to take a break – they knew it was a lost cause when he was like this."*

Instead of telling the reader that Peter neglects his personal relationships even more, the writer might describe his tendency to cancel plans with friends and family, or his lack of communication with them when he is wrapped up in a case.

Example: *"Peter's phone was filled with missed calls and messages from his family and friends, but he barely had time to look at them. He was so focused on the case"*

Instead of telling the reader that Peter becomes more critical of himself, the writer might describe his tendency to second-guess his decisions and his tendency to blame himself for any setbacks or mistakes.

Example: *"Peter sat at his desk, staring at the case file in front of him. He had made a mistake, and it was eating at him. He couldn't believe he had missed something so obvious."*

ACT 3:

Here are some examples of "show, don't tell" in act 3:

Instead of telling the reader that Peter begins to re-evaluate his priorities, the writer might describe his actions as he starts to make an effort to balance his work and personal life, such as taking time off to spend with his family or making an effort to stay in touch with friends.

Example: *"Peter sat at the dinner table, surrounded by his family. It had been too long since he had taken a break from work, and he was determined to make up for it. He had spent the day cooking and playing with his kids, and he was enjoying himself more than he had in a long time."*

Instead of telling the reader that Peter becomes more confident in his abilities as a detective, the writer might describe his newfound confidence as he approaches cases and makes decisions with assurance and clarity.

Example: *"Peter stood in the conference room, looking at the case board in front of him. He had been working on this case for weeks, and he was starting to see the pieces fall into place. He confidently gave an update and the case was solved"*

Using "show, don't tell" in writing can help to create a more immersive and engaging reading experience, and can also help to reveal character and plot in a more subtle and effective way. It is a useful technique for writers to keep in mind when crafting their stories and characters.

If your character is scared, don't SAY they are scared, SHOW they are scared.

Fear
Here is an example of a male in a crime novel feeling scared for his life:

"I don't know what you want from me, but please just let me go. I promise I won't say anything to anyone, I just want to go home."

"I've told you everything I know, I swear. Please, just let me go. I have a family to think about."

"I'll do whatever you want, just don't hurt me. Please, I'll give you whatever you want, just let me go."

Can you see? We can visualise more clearly his thoughts and feelings. We feel more immersed as the reader, which pulls them into you story.

Sadness
Here are some examples of dialogue for a man who is distraught after losing his best friend to a murder:
Instead of just saying 'he is sad', you can pull your readers in with the following:

"I can't believe he's gone. We've been best friends since we were kids, how am I supposed to go on without him?"

"I keep expecting him to walk through the door, or to see a message from him on my phone. It's like my brain can't accept that he's really gone."

"I keep replaying the last time I saw him in my head, wondering if there was anything I could have done differently. I can't shake the feeling that this is my fault."

Guilt
Instead of writing 'the man felt guilty for not being there for his wife when she got some bad news'
Instead write:

"I can't believe I wasn't there for you when you needed me most. I'm so sorry, I just had to finish up this project at work and I didn't realise how much time had passed."

"I feel like the worst husband in the world. I should have dropped everything and come home as soon as you called. How can you ever forgive me?"

"I keep thinking about how alone you must have felt when you heard the news.

It's my job to protect and support you, and I failed you. I don't know how to make it up to you."

Happiness

Here are three examples of dialogue for a woman who has just found out she got her dream job:

"I can't believe it! I got the job! I've been dreaming of working at XYZ company for years, and now it's finally happening!"

"I'm so excited, I don't even know what to do with myself! Thank you for helping me prepare for the interview, I couldn't have done it without you."

"I can't wait to start my new job and see where it takes me. This is exactly the opportunity I've been waiting for, and I'm going to make the most of it."

Relief

Instead of just writing 'she felt relieved,' here are three examples of dialogue for a woman who is relieved after her little girl was found safe:

"Thank goodness you're safe! I was so worried when I couldn't find you, I didn't know what to do."

"I'm just so relieved that you're okay. I can't even imagine how scared you must have been when you were lost."

"I'm so sorry I panicked. I just love you so much and couldn't bear the thought of anything happening to you. I'm just so grateful you're safe."

If you sprinkle in dialogue and show-not-tell with their body language, you're onto a winner and your readers will be there in the story with you!

Here are some ideas of body language that could be used to show that the mother is relieved after her little girl was found safe:

- She embraces her daughter tightly, tears streaming down her face
- She sinks to the ground, her legs giving out from relief
- She covers her face with her hands, sobbing with relief
- She embraces the person who found her daughter, thanking them profusely
- She giggles with relief, hugging her daughter and kissing her forehead
- She stares at her daughter in disbelief, as if she can't believe that she's really safe
- She wraps her arms around her daughter protectively, as if she never wants to let go again.

Then add in the dialogue, so mixed together it would be:

She sinks to the ground, her legs giving out from relief. "I'm so sorry I panicked. I just love you so much and couldn't bear the thought of anything happening to you. I'm just so grateful you're safe."

Can you see how that is so much better than just writing 'She was relieved'.

Let's try another of our examples and mixing them together. Remember the woman who was happy she got her dream job?

Here's some ideas of **SHOWING** how she could act (not telling):

- She pumps her fist in the air, a triumphant grin on her face
- She jumps up and down, letting out a squeal of joy
- She wraps her arms around herself, hugging herself tightly
- She covers her face with her hands, tears of joy streaming down her face
- She dances around the room, unable to contain her excitement

- She throws her arms around the person she's talking to, hugging them tightly.
- She clasps her hands together, a look of pure joy on her face.

If we now pick one, mix it in with the dialogue we get:

She jumps up and down, letting out a squeal of joy, "I'm so excited, I don't even know what to do with myself! Thank you for helping me prepare for the interview, I couldn't have done it without you!"

How much better is that rather than just 'she was excited about getting a new job'.

15

Creating Compelling Villains

There are several ways that writers can make a villain more compelling in a novel:

Give the villain depth and complexity:

Villains who are complex and multifaceted, with their own motivations, values, and beliefs, can be more compelling to readers. Rather than making the villain one-dimensional or simple, give them depth and complexity to make them more interesting and believable.

Make the villain relatable:

Villains who are relatable, even in small ways, can be more compelling to readers. By giving the villain some humanising qualities or vulnerabilities, writers can make them more believable and make it easier for readers to understand their motivations.

Give the villain a clear and compelling motivation:

A villain with a clear and compelling motivation can be more interesting and engaging to readers. Rather than making the villain's actions seem arbitrary or random, give them a clear and understandable reason for their actions.

Show the villain's perspective:

By showing the villain's perspective and giving readers a glimpse into their thoughts and feelings, writers can make them more complex and relatable. This can help readers understand the villain's motivations and make them more compelling.

Avoid making the villain too evil:

Villains who are too evil or one-dimensional can be less compelling to readers. By avoiding overly evil or cartoonish villains, writers can create more believable and engaging antagonists.

By following these tips, writers can create more compelling and interesting villains in their novels.

16

Writing Dialogue For Characters In A Novel

Here are a few tips for writing dialogue for characters in a novel:

Make the dialogue authentic and realistic: Dialogue should sound natural and authentic, and should reflect the character's personality, background, and circumstances.

Use dialogue to reveal character: Dialogue can be a powerful tool for revealing a character's personality, values, beliefs, and motivations. Use dialogue to reveal character through what characters say and how they say it.

Use dialogue to advance the plot: Dialogue can be used to advance the plot and reveal important information to the reader. Use dialogue to reveal plot twists, reveal character motivations, or move the story forward.

Vary the length and rhythm of dialogue: Vary the length and rhythm of dialogue to keep it interesting and engaging. Avoid too much long-winded or expositional dialogue, and mix up the pace and flow of the conversation.

Use body language and gestures: Use body language and gestures to add depth and richness to the dialogue. Body language and gestures can reveal a character's emotions, attitudes, and intentions.

By following these tips, writers can effectively use dialogue to bring their characters to life and create a more immersive and engaging reading experience.

17

Examples Of Regrets Your Characters Might Have

A character with regrets makes them more relatable and human, as it is a universal experience to have regrets. It adds depth and complexity to a character, and allows the reader to understand and empathise with their choices and actions. It also makes the character more vulnerable as they are showing a weakness or flaw, which makes them more realistic and dynamic. Additionally, a character's regrets can drive the plot and conflict in a novel, as they may attempt to make amends for past mistakes or be forced to confront them in some way.

Some possible regrets a character might have are as follows:

- Not pursuing a passion or dream earlier in life
- Not traveling or experiencing new cultures more
- Not taking better care of one's physical or mental health
- Not investing in oneself (e.g. education or self-improvement)
- Not taking risks or being too afraid to fail
- Not spending enough time with loved ones or friends
- Not expressing gratitude or appreciation enough to others

- Not living in the present moment and enjoying it
- Not taking the time to reflect and learn from past mistakes
- Not standing up for oneself or allowing oneself to be treated poorly

Using a character's regrets in a novel can make the plot more compelling in several ways:

- Regrets can serve as a source of inner conflict for the character, making them question their past actions and choices, and potentially leading them to make different decisions in the present.

- Regrets can also be used to create external conflict, as the character may be forced to confront the consequences of their past actions and deal with the people or situations they have hurt.

- A character's regrets can also be used to create a sense of tension and suspense, as the reader may wonder how the character will deal with their regrets and whether they will be able to find redemption.

- Regrets can also add a theme to the story, that is about redemption, forgiveness, second chance, etc.

- A character's regrets can also be used to reveal important information about the character's backstory, motivations, and personality, which can deepen the reader's understanding of the character and the story as a whole.

- It can also be used as a plot twist, where the reader gets to know that the character actually regrets something that they have not revealed to anyone else yet.

18

Lists Of Flaws, Weaknesses And Strengths

Flaws

Selfishness
Dishonesty
Envy
Arrogance
Greed
Laziness
Jealousy
Anger
Hubris
Impulsiveness
Insecurity
Intolerance
Narcissism
Obstinacy
Prejudice
Self-centredness
Stubbornness
Vanity

Vengefulness
Wrath
Procrastination
Close-mindedness
Cowardice
Deceitfulness
Ingratitude
Manipulativeness
Pessimism
Self-doubt
Self-indulgence
Unreliability

Which of these character flaws is speaking to you for one of your characters? Write it down.

Weaknessess

Addiction
Apathy
Arrogance
Cowardice
Cynicism
Dependence
Depression
Desperation
Disorganisation
Egocentrism
Fear
Gullibility
Hatred
Ignorance
Immaturity
Impulsiveness
Inferiority complex
Insecurity

Jealousy
Loneliness
Malice
Obsession
Overconfidence
Perfectionism
Pessimism
Prejudice
Self-doubt
Self-sabotage
Stubbornness
Weak-willed

Which of these are speaking to you? Write it down.

Strengths

Ambition
Brave
Caring
Compassionate
Confident
Conscientious
Cooperative
Courageous
Creative
Determined
Diligent
Empathetic
Flexible
Forgiving
Generous
Humble
Honest
Humorous
Imaginative

Independent
Innovative
Inventive
Kind
Loyal
Open-minded
Optimistic
Persistent
Responsible
Self-disciplined
Thoughtful

Keep these strengths in mind for your character throughout the story to help them with their flaws/battles.

19

Creating Your Character Arc Using Flaws, Weaknesses And Strengths - The Easy Way!

In this chapter you will find a list of negative traits and their opposites.

Why have we included this?

Simply put, you will be able to create a character arc with them.

Start with:
ACT 1 – the negative trait
ACT 2 – the changing
ACT 3 is the opposite to ACT 1

Negative: Selfish - **Positive:** Altruistic

Negative: Lazy - **Positive:** Diligent

Negative: Greedy - **Positive:** Generous

Negative: Dishonest - **Positive:** Honest

Negative: Arrogant - **Positive:** Humble

Negative: Vengeful - **Positive:** Forgiving

Negative: Intolerant - **Positive:** Tolerant

Negative: Cowardly - **Positive:** Brave

Negative: Unreliable - **Positive:** Dependable

Negative: Close-minded - **Positive:** Open-minded

Negative: Angry - **Positive:** Calm

Negative: Impulsive - **Positive:** Thoughtful

Negative: Prejudiced - **Positive:** Objective

Negative: Self-centred - **Positive:** Altruistic

Negative: Envious - **Positive:** Content

Negative: Pessimistic - **Positive:** Optimistic

Negative: Stubborn - **Positive:** Flexible

Negative: Insecure - **Positive:** Confident

Negative: Narcissistic - **Positive:** Humorous

Negative: Procrastinating - **Positive:** Proactive

Negative: Manipulative - **Positive:** Honest

Negative: Malicious - **Positive:** Kind

Negative: Self-doubting - **Positive:** Self-assured

Negative: Self-indulgent - **Positive:** Self-disciplined

Negative: Unforgiving - **Positive:** Forgiving

Negative: Gossiping - **Positive:** Discrete

Negative: Disrespectful - **Positive:** Respectful

Negative: Disorganised - **Positive:** Organised

Negative: Egotistical - **Positive:** Humble

Negative: Ingratitude - **Positive:** Grateful

20

Taking It One Step Further

Let's use an example of a main character going from:

Greedy to generous

How would that look in a story?

THIS IS how we make our characters come alive.

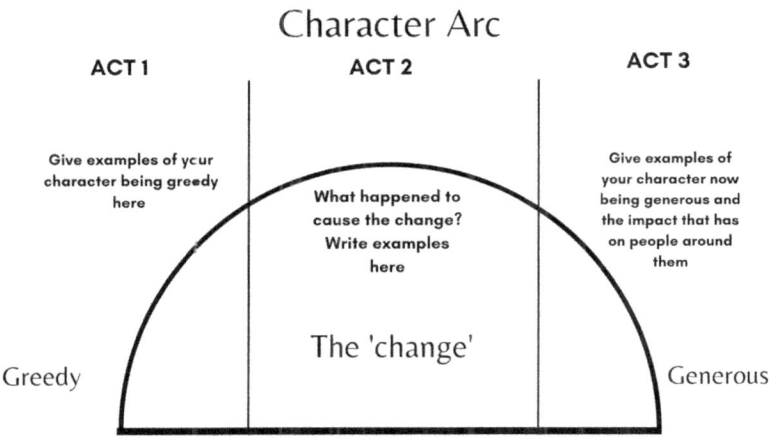

In Act 1 – Give actual examples of their everyday life showing them being greedy and how it makes others feel – the impact.

In Act 2 – What was the single event/string of events that caused that character to start to change? Give examples of the impact.

In Act 3 – Give examples using show not tell of your character slowly adopting this new trait and the impact on characters around them.

Let's go one step further to help you with *show not tell* for a few examples:

Our example of greedy-generous for a character arc.

Negative: Greedy

Examples of someone being greedy:

- They are never satisfied with what they have and always want more.
- They hoard resources and don't share with others.
- They engage in unethical behaviour, such as fraud or embezzlement, in order to acquire more wealth or power.

Positive: Generous

Examples of someone being generous:

- They are always willing to give their time, money, or resources to help others.
- They go out of their way to help people in need and make a positive impact on the community.
- They are always happy to share what they have with others and are grateful for their blessing.

This is how it would look:

We can now see how that character will change and the 'change' will be compelling!

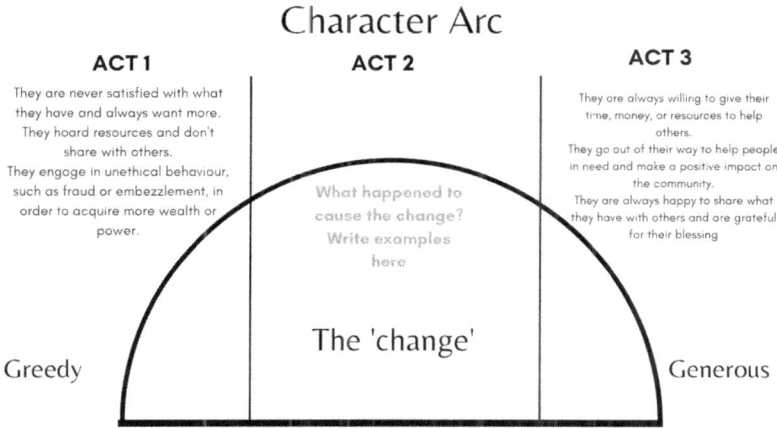

What would make a character 'change' - Act 2?

There are several ways a character may change in a novel. Here are a few examples:

Personal Experience: The character may have a life-changing experience that leads them to see the world differently. For example, they may experience poverty or lose everything they hold dear, which causes them to understand the struggles of others and become more empathetic.

Meeting a positive role model: The character may come across someone who embodies generosity and selflessness, which inspires them to change their ways.

Change of heart: The character may have a moral or emotional awakening that leads them to realise the negative impact of their greed on themselves and others. They may come to regret their past actions and want to make amends.

External Pressure: The character may face external pressure to change such as societal or legal consequences of their actions. They may be forced to face the reality of their greed and feel compelled to change for self-preservation

Personal Growth: The character may change through a process of personal growth, where they learn and develop new skills and understanding, leading them to rethink their values, ideals and attitude.

Let's take it one step further…

How does our character arc look now?

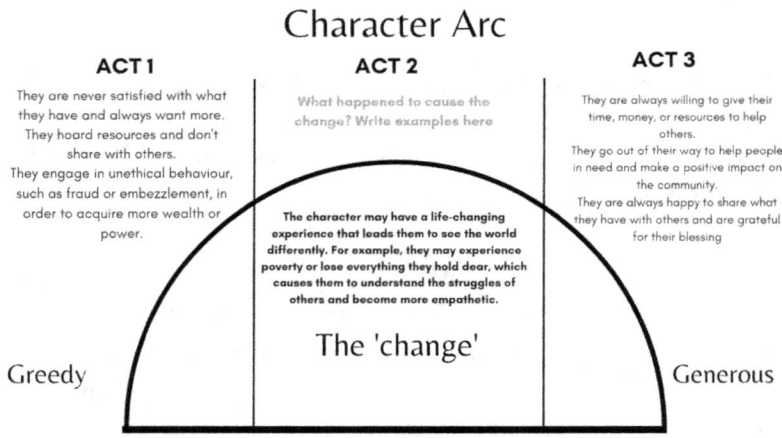

How will your character respond to the conflict or having to 'change'?

People can respond to conflict in many different ways, and their response may be influenced by a variety of factors, including their personality, past experiences, and the specific circumstances of the conflict. Here are a few examples of how people may respond to conflict and some possible reasons for their response:

Avoidance: Some people may avoid conflict altogether, choosing to ignore or sidestep the issue rather than confront it directly. They may do this because they fear confrontation, want to avoid potential hurt feelings, or lack the skills to handle the conflict effectively.

Compromise: Others may be willing to compromise in order to find a middle ground and reach a resolution that both parties can live with. They may do this because they value relationships and are willing to make sacrifices to maintain them, or they have a cooperative mindset and seek to find common ground.

Collaboration: Some individuals may seek to work with others to find a mutually beneficial solution, they might be people who values teamwork and collaboration, they might be highly communicative people that is a good listener and they value everyone's input.

Accommodation: Some people may choose to put the needs of the other person before their own, even if it means giving up what they want. This can be due to feeling guilty, a sense of obligation or an inclination to be accommodating or too kind.

Competition: Some people may approach conflict as a competition, seeking to assert their own needs and wants over those of the other person. They may do this because they want to win, don't want to lose, want to be in control or feel like they are the only one that know what's the best.

Confrontation: Some people may respond to conflict by being direct and assertive, taking a confrontational stance. They may do this because they believe that direct communication is the most effective way to handle the conflict, they might be extroverted people that like to express themselves, they might be people that believe in direct and honest communication.

It's worth mentioning that people may use different approaches to conflict depending on the situation and people involved, and it's not uncommon for people to use different approach during different stages of a conflict as well. Understanding the motivations behind different ways of responding to conflict can be useful in understanding the behaviour of the characters in a novel or people in real-life.

21

Resources

To help you with your character building, I've got you started with the negatives and positive examples:

Negative: Selfish

Examples of someone being selfish:

- They only think about their own needs and wants, and don't consider the needs of others.
- They are unwilling to share resources or help others, even when it would be easy to do so.
- They prioritise their own well-being above the well-being of others, even to the point of harm.

Positive: Altruistic

Examples of someone being altruistic:

- They are always willing to lend a helping hand and don't hesitate to put others needs before their own.
- They often volunteer their time and resources to help

those less fortunate.
- They take great satisfaction in helping others and truly value their contributions to the community.

Negative: Lazy

Examples of someone being lazy:

- They have trouble getting started on tasks and often procrastinate.
- They have a hard time sticking to plans and projects, and frequently give up prematurely.
- They make excuses for their lack of effort and don't take responsibility for their shortcomings.

Positive: Diligent

Examples of someone being diligent:

- They take great care in their work, paying close attention to detail.
- They set high standards for themselves and strive to meet them.
- They persist in their efforts, even in the face of adversity or setbacks.

Negative: Greedy

Examples of someone being greedy:

- They are never satisfied with what they have and always want more.
- They hoard resources and don't share with others.

- They engage in unethical behavior, such as fraud or embezzlement, in order to acquire more wealth or power.

Positive: Generous

Examples of someone being generous:

- They are always willing to give their time, money, or resources to help others.
- They go out of their way to help people in need and make a positive impact on the community.
- They are always happy to share what they have with others and are grateful for their blessings.

Negative: Dishonest

Examples of someone being dishonest:

- They tell lies or exaggerate the truth in order to gain an advantage.
- They take credit for the work of others.
- They hide information that might be detrimental to their interests.

Positive: Honest

Examples of someone being honest:

- They tell the truth, even when it's difficult or inconvenient.
- They admit when they are wrong or have made a mistake
- They are reliable and trustworthy in their words and actions.

Negative: Arrogant

Examples of someone being arrogant:

- They think they are better than others and look down on them.
- They don't listen to others or take their opinions seriously.
- They act superior and entitled.

Positive: Humble

Examples of someone being humble:

- They have a clear understanding of their own limitations and are always willing to learn.
- They respect the opinions of others and give credit where credit is due.
- They remain grounded and modest despite any accomplishments or successes they may achieve

Character Occupations

Doctor
Lawyer
Engineer
Teacher
Nurse
IT Professional
Salesperson
Artist
Police Officer
Firefighter
Accountant

Chef
Electrician
Plumber
Construction Worker
Mechanic
Retail Worker
Delivery Driver
Social Worker
Receptionist
Janitor
Security Guard
Cleaner
Landscaper
Hairdresser
Barber
Dentist
Veterinarian
Librarian
Museum Curator
Secretary
Bookkeeper
Banker
Real Estate Agent
Travel Agent
Insurance Agent
Stockbroker
Postal Worker
Paralegal
Locksmith
Carpenter
Gardener
Baker
Farmer
Fisherman
Photographer
Writer
Musician

Actor
Dancer
Comedian
Athlete
Coach
Personal Trainer
Programmer
Systems Analyst
Web Developer
Graphic Designer
Market Researcher
Public Relations Specialist

Obviously, there are many more, but this is just to get you started!

List Of Vices

Smoking
Drinking alcohol
Gambling
Drug use
Overeating
Shopping addiction
Internet addiction
Pornography addiction

List Of Good Habits

Does your character do any of these?

Regular exercise and physical activity
Eating a healthy and balanced diet
Getting enough sleep

Practicing good hygiene
Maintaining a positive attitude and mindset
Practicing stress management techniques (e.g. meditation, yoga, deep breathing)
Being organised and keeping a schedule
Reading, learning, and continuing education
Building and maintaining relationships with friends and family
Setting and working towards goals, and having a sense of purpose.

Physical Features

Hair colour and texture: blonde, brunette, curly, straight, etc.

Eye colour: brown, blue, green, grey, etc.

Skin colour and texture: fair, olive, dark, smooth, rough, etc.

Facial features: sharp nose, full lips, pointy ears, almond-shaped eyes, etc.

Height and build: tall, short, slim, athletic, etc

Body hair: thick, thin, coarse, fine, etc.

Hands and feet: long fingers, big toes, calloused hands, etc.

Fingerprints and other unique characteristics: whorls, loops, arches, moles, etc

Posture and gait: slouched, upright, limps, etc

Voice: deep, high-pitched, raspy, etc

This list is not exhaustive and there are many other physical features that can be considered, but these are some examples of the types of physical characteristics that can be used to describe an individual.

22

Your Full Character Profile Ready To Go

Here is a list of questions you can use to fully develop a character profile for your novel. You should have all the answers to fill it in from this book.

Basic Information

What is the character's name?
What is the character's age?
What is the character's occupation?
What is the character's physical appearance?
What is the character's personality like?
What is the character's background?
What is the character's family situation?

Positive Traits

What are the character's strengths?
What are the character's positive characteristics?

What are the character's talents?
What are the character's good habits?
What are the character's values?
What are the character's aspirations?
What does the character care about?

Negative Traits

What are the character's weaknesses?
What are the character's negative characteristics?
What are the character's bad habits?
What are the character's fears?
What are the character's regrets?
What are the character's vices?

Internal Motivations

What does the character want?
What drives the character?
What are the character's goals?
What is the character's motivation?
What are the character's needs?
What are the character's desires?
What are the character's beliefs?

External Motivations

What are the character's relationships like?
Who are the character's allies and enemies?
What are the character's influences?
What are the character's experiences?
How does the character respond to conflict?
How does the character respond to challenges?

How Does The Character Deal With Change?

Act 1:

How will the character act in act 1? (Hint: A good place to start is their negative trait)
What will the character's role be in act 1?
What are the character's goals in act 1?
What are the character's main conflicts in act 1?

Reasons for Change:

Why does the character change throughout the story?
What events or experiences trigger the change?
How does the change affect the character's actions and relationships?
What is the final outcome of the character's change?

Act 2:

How will the character act in act 2?
What will the character's role be in act 2?
What are the character's goals in act 2?
What are the character's main conflicts in act 2?

Act 3:

How will the character act in act 3?
What will the character's role be in act 3?
What are the character's goals in act 3?
What are the character's main conflicts in act 3?

It's important to note that these questions should be answered for each individual character you are creating and as you write the story, you might find that you need to adjust the character's profile as well. Remember that the development of the character is a fluid process, and depending on the story arc, the character may change during the story.

Conclusion

In conclusion, writing compelling characters and using vivid dialogue is crucial for creating a successful and impactful work of fiction. By using character arcs, we can show the growth and development of our characters over time, which helps to make them feel more real and relatable to our readers.

The ongoing process of character development is also important for us as writers, as it helps us to continually learn and grow in our craft. By focusing on creating well-rounded and engaging characters, we can give our readers a more enjoyable and meaningful reading experience. So, keep working on your character development skills and keep learning and growing as a writer – it will benefit you and make your books even better for your readers!

Our Range Of Novel Planning Workbooks

YES! You CAN write a Novel.

Now you've got your incredible characters sorted, let's get that novel written…

Introducing the ultimate tool for aspiring writers.

Unlock a million possibilities and become a master storyteller in any genre with our comprehensive novel outline workbook.

Our **done-for-you template** guides you through the writing process step by step, providing expert tips and tricks along the way.

Craft an unforgettable plot, create captivating characters with clear arcs, and bring your world to life with our help.

Whether you're a beginner or an experienced writer, our workbook is designed to help you take your writing to the next level.

From world building to crafting exciting endings and unexpected plot twists, we've got you covered.

And when it's time to publish, we'll provide a **winning strategy** for creating an eye-catching book cover, a captivating blurb, and a professional-sounding synopsis.

Don't wait any longer to unleash your creativity and start your journey towards writing success.

Order now and let's turn your words into a captivating story that **readers will love**.

If you want to grab a copy now, simply type in *"How To Write A*

Winning Fiction Book Outline by Hackney and Jones" on your online shopping platform of choice.

If you loved this book and feel ready to start writing, check out our full range of novel outline workbooks to get you started on your journey. Can't see one in your genre? Visit our website at **hackneyandjones.com** to see our complete range.

www.ingramcontent.com/pod-product-compliance
Lightning Source LLC
Chambersburg PA
CBHW050031130526
44590CB00042B/2437